It's probably true that most folks come to Sidmouth to sit on the sea front rather than to go walking. However there are always those with energy to burn who tire of passive pursuits. This little book is for those restless souls (or is it soles?) with itchy feet who feel the need to explore

their immediate surroundings. The walks are not long route marches (particularly the flat town trail) but they will gainfully occupy those who enjoy a stroll lasting a few hours or so.

Should you need a map, the OS 'Explorer 30' covers the area.

Sidmouth is nestled in a deep, steep valley so it's inevitable that there will be some steep gradients, up and down. By the same token the efforts put in to climb such steep slopes will be rewarded with terrific views. Much has been written about the elegant setting of this Regency resort and the best way to see if the writers' statements are true is to do these circular walks. Three of the outings start and finish at the excellent Tourist Information Centre, at the swimming pool in Ham Lane, located near the eastern end of the Esplanade, whilst the other two commence a few miles away. We begin by breaking you in gently!

1: A Short Sidmouth Town Trail

This town trail is not too taxing, with nothing more than the occasional slope to negotiate. The walk is intended to give you an idea of some of the history and heritage of the resort and, perhaps, draw your attention to things you might miss if just wandering about.

From the entrance to the Tourist Information Centre and swimming pool cut through to the Ham, the lawned area beside the Sid (there used to be a gasworks here), and walk to the eastern end of the sea front. Depending on the season, you may see fishing boats on the beach. Turn right and walk westwards along the sea front as far as the end of the Bedford Hotel. But before we arrive there, drink in the views and savour the special atmosphere that is Sidmouth, and you will appreciate you are here in Devon's classiest resort. If you ever see a film called *A Summer Story*, based on 'The Apple Tree', a short story by John Galsworthy (who wrote *The Forsyte Saga*), then you might recognise the buildings on your right as, in the film, the part of 'Torquay' was played by Sidmouth!

Sidmouth, by courtesy of the excellent Sid Vale Association, the oldest conservation society in the country, is a town with many blue plaques placed on its notable buildings. These give details of the history behind them. Several appear on our right side. The first we see is on the western end of the Royal York and Faulkner Hotel and there are two more in quick succession on the architecturally pleasing Beach House and Mocha Restaurant. The history of these and most of the other buildings passed on the walk can be found in another of my books, *Sidmouth Past & Present,* an ideal companion to this book.

We now pass three more hotels, the Elizabeth, the Devoran and the Kingswood, which also has a blue plaque to tell you that it was originally the Marine Baths. Invalids coming to Sidmouth could enjoy a range of treatments: mud packs, electrical treatments, seaweed baths and so on. Where the baths were is now the hotel's restaurant. In the summer the fronts of these hotels are beautifully garlanded in flowers, a really impressive sight.

Just beyond is the Riviera Hotel and then the Bedford Hotel, where we turn right into Station Road to leave the sea front. On our right is No 1 Bedford Place, with a nameplate saying 'Locomotion'. The station in this road is at the far end of it and it is rumoured that it was deliberately kept as far out of town as possible to discourage 'the hordes'; such visitors should have been put off by the hike into town or the weary one back up to the station at the end of a beach day. The line was a branch which left the Otter valley near Tipton St John to climb through Harpford Woods and on into Sidmouth.

The last building, of this run, on our right is Abbeyfield Court but if you look at the upper part of it you will see, etched in stone, 'Torbay View' from the days when it, too, was a hotel. On the opposite side of the road is the fine cricket field, with thatched pavilion. Some famous people have played here, including the creator of Sherlock Holmes, Sir Arthur Conan Doyle.

On our right is the Triangle, where buses regularly arrive and leave. There are also toilets here if needed. Beyond is the putting green, fringed by the occasional palm tree, a reminder of the mild climate enjoyed down in this deep hollow.

Stay with Station Road for the time being. To the left is the impressive run of buildings of Fortfield Terrace, complete with its double-headed eagle high on number 8. This was put here in 1831 to commemorate the visit of Grand Duchess Helene of Russia, who arrived in the resort with a staff of over a hundred people. The following year the property was leased by Mr Barrett, whose daughter was with him. She, of course, later became Elizabeth Barrett-Browning. When you do this walk you will be walking in the footsteps of the rich, the titled and the famous.

Beyond the Triangle it will be necessary to cross the road in order to find a pavement. In the next hundred yards or so the entrance to the Fortfield Hotel will be passed, as will a smaller hotel on your left, Cranmere House. Keen Dartmoor walkers will know that this hotel's namesake is Cranmere Pool on Dartmoor, an empty tarn where the first Dartmoor 'letterbox' was set up. If your curiosity is aroused then you should read my book about Cranmere Pool.

A little farther up the road, and past the Arts Centre, we reach a pedestrian crossing which we cross. Just beyond it turn right and proceed down Coburg Road. If you are a fan of the type of architecture known as 'cottage *orné*' then you will enjoy this thoroughfare. The name of the road derives from the death of the Duke of Kent at Sidmouth in 1820. He held estates in Coburg and his wife was the daughter of the Duke of Saxe-Coburg-Saalfeld.

Stay with this road, past the tennis courts, to reach its end by Sidmouth's wonderful museum. A plaque on the building tells us about Stephen Reynolds, a champion of fishermen, who achieved fame with his book *A Poor Man's House*. The clock on the side of the museum was placed to mark the 150th anniversary (1846–1996) of the Sid Vale Association.

At the museum we pass around a small corner into Church Street. If you have time to visit the church do so, because it's a lovely building. If not, head on down Church Street where there are still many family businesses trading, like those at the

furniture shop, the butcher, the florist, the toy shop, the ironmongers and so on. This straight road, which has won awards for its appearance (see the plaque near Haymans the butchers), will take you down into the Market Square, the heart of the town centre, which was 'enhanced' in 1990.

Turn left and walk up the gently sloped Old Fore Street, which is pedestrianised apart from access for delivery vehicles, so don't be too casual! There are a few pubs in this street should you be thirsty. The Old Ship Inn, built in 1350, towards the top of the street and on the left hand side, bears yet another blue plaque.

We now reach the High Street and, staying on the left side of the road, we pass the long-established furniture firm of Potbury's who seem to like 5 as a number for their telephone! Beyond that, Lloyd's Bank has a distinct architectural style and, not to be outdone, so has Barclay's Bank slightly farther up the road on the opposite side. Just as the road starts to kink left we reach the Methodist Church. Just before it we turn left into Church Lane, purely a pedestrian thoroughfare.

This takes us behind Potbury's and other shops. On our right is a red brick wall which becomes, for a short distance, a wall of boulders. Here there is a low entrance/exit which we pass through to reach a park. Immediately bear right and follow the wall for about 30 yards until the path curves left by some benches. On the first is a dedication: "Presented by Sidmouth Young Hoteliers in loving memory of Kitcheners' Music Clubs, 1967–69 'The Song is ended but the Melody lingers on'". Stay with the line of direction to pass a small shelter and the next bench with a more typical dedication "In Memory of Philip George Tippett and Tuppenny, September 21st 1973".

From this point head under the adjacent tree and straight across the grass, if it's not too wet, and into another part of the Blackmore Gardens through a breach in the pebble wall.

From here the Old Chancel, once the home of one of Sidmouth's greatest characters, Peter Orlando Hutchinson, is seen beyond the bowling green. We now head right on a fairly straight path. Should you need a rest the wall has been adapted into a bench, such is the popularity of this 'oasis' in Sidmouth. There are a couple of non-blue plaques to look out for here. One is to the loving memory of Mrs W. M. Brown "whose kindness created this garden" and beside it another more recent one placed by Rotary International saying "Scented garden for the Blind established by the Rotary Club of Sidmouth to commemorate the Silver Jubilee of Her Majesty Queen Elizabeth II, 2nd June 1977".

Stay with the path which takes you out of the Blackmore Gardens at a point where the distinctively gabled May Terrace is reached. Opposite is the Sidmouth Victoria Cottage Hospital, which was founded in 1896. May Cottage, on our right, was the earlier cottage hospital and is now the home of an international school.

Once more we our back in the traffic and at the junction of All Saints Road, Radway and the top end of the High Street. On the right hand corner is the Old Meeting, a building with a history.

Follow the pavement around the corner on which it stands and proceed back down the High Street.

This time the Methodist Church is on our right. Just before it is a block of shops with curved arches now filled in. Part of this was originally the Grand Cinema. Stay with the High Street. Just past Woolworth, also on the left hand side of the road, is Shipton's, cutters and mounters of precise stones, which bears yet another blue plaque.

The road now divides and as we have already 'explored' Old Fore Street we can now stroll along plain Fore Street. This road can become very congested when a number of lorries deliver at the same time!

Stay with the road past the front of the Black Horse and then turn left into East Street. With no more plaques to be read, make your way back to the start and a well-earned rest!

2: To Salcombe Regis and Back Again!

There are various schools of thought on the subject of whether it's better to begin a walk with the toughest mile or end one with it. If you follow this route you have little choice but to gird up your loins, take a deep breath and cope, as best you can, with the dizzy slopes which await you. There are compensations. If it's a cool day it will warm you up and if it's a warm day you will have every justification for stopping to enjoy the vistas at any, or at all, of the vantage points!

Make your way from the Tourist Information Centre to the end of the Esplanade, where the River Sid discharges into the sea as it passes through the beach. This is where this walk, of about four miles, begins and ends.

The first thing we do is to cross the historic Alma Bridge, named after a battle in the Crimean War. To our right there are signs warning of falling rocks but, despite this, some silly people persist in visiting the beach beyond. The cliff-line is gradually receding and gives us a different start to the walk we could have experienced some years ago. You can either walk up the 102 steps or take the less direct winding path to the same point where the previous path is fenced off. The rockfalls have necessitated an inland detour before we can rejoin the coast higher up Salcombe Hill Cliff.

On reaching a road it's necessary to walk uphill along the pavement, parallel with, but out of sight of, the coast and it's not a major surprise to discover that this is Cliff Road. The road bends

around to eventually climb past Coastguard Cottage. A red brick wall here runs up to another lane on the right. Follow it, past the Rocket House and Heathlands, and the cliff will soon be regained again. Although we have climbed steadily ever since the start of the walk it should be noted that we are only on the 'nursery slopes' of the great Salcombe Hill. Our way upwards is now within the restriction of a low wire fence, whilst to the right the bushes have been blown into a rigid, uniform angle by the constant onshore sea breezes (and not the prevailing wind as some are told when walking along here).

Just before we enter some woodland there are a few benches with recuperative qualities, for the view back over Sidmouth, and along the coast towards Ladram Bay, is a fine one. It's possible, for those in the know, to pick out Fortfield Terrace, the Connaught Gardens and other buildings, whilst those with good eyesight will easily spot the parish church way below.

The hill gets steeper on its upper slopes but the effort made to scale the bevelled summit is energy well spent. You will know when you have reached this point because you emerge from

the woods to reach a signpost with a bench, to the memory of Harry Patrick Llewellyn Langmead (1897–1971), immediately behind it. Why not take five minutes out to savour the surroundings and the fine view of the lower Sid Valley? You fully deserve it.

Here there is a choice of routes, for other walkers, but our chosen path is the one pointing to 'Salcombe Mouth'. The going is now much easier as in about 40 yards we reach a gateway. Beside it, on the left side, is a short ladder, a piece of mild geriatric gymnastic equipment, to take curious walkers up to a mini-monument. This piece of cliff-top furniture is here to inform us what can be seen all around this landscape.

Pass through the gate, to the right of this feature, and note this other 'landmark', which looks like a tombstone, just inside of it. Ahead, and for about a hundred yards, is almost level ground. We make the most of it by easily strolling along to the next gate. Just beyond it is a small isolated stone referred to as the 'Frog Stone'. Its presence here would probably appear to be a fine example of the eccentricity of the English. This flinty-looking outcrop was airlifted here from its original location at Hook Ebb Reef. A light-hearted request by the Sid Vale Association resulted in a naval helicopter winching it into position in 1964 – the 'swinging sixties' when 'rock' arrived!

Below is an enormous depression in the landscape, one of a number along this coast towards Beer. Although it's a terrific coastline, it's a demanding one because of the ups and downs along the way. The Sidmouth to Seaton path is a real 'killer'!

So, at this Frog Stone, don't go headlong down into the mighty chasm, Salcombe Mouth, but turn inland and walk along and above the fence which runs along the contour. At the first gate it's a case of 'one step forward, four steps back' as it swings against us and we have to reverse in order to advance.

Proceed along the level path to the next gate which, for a change, happens to be going our way.

A broad track now appears coming up the hillside on our right and cuts across our path. We head straight across to pass through a kissing gate and over the trunk of a tree to immediately reach another crossroads of

paths. This time we turn downhill towards Salcombe Regis, half a mile away.

The path descends steeply through a coniferous plantation to meet yet another, but more level, path coming in from the right. We turn left onto it and follow it, inland, to a point where it meets a surfaced road on the edge of Salcombe Regis. On reaching it walk up the hill to reach the church's car park. Here there is an information board about the East Devon Heritage Coast which imparts plenty of information about the geology and that the National Trust still operate the quarry at nearby Dunscombe, specifically for stone to repair and restore Exeter Cathedral.

Arthur Mee included this as part of his entry for the village in his 1938 book, *Devon*: "There are among the records of Salcombe also the interesting record of three farms once held by Saxon kings; they passed from the kings into the possession of Exeter Cathedral, and after that, about the time of Waterloo, they passed to George Cornish, in whose family they remain to this day – three transfers of land in nearly 12 centuries. One more notable record we came upon here is of an 18th century vicar who was at the church for 63 years."

"An attractive and in some ways a primitive place, with a glorious sea view from the gate, the church has a 15th century tower but much of it is older. A Norman arch can be seen outside the chancel wall, and a carved stone inside may have been its lintel. The arches on both sides of the nave are 13th century, but those on the north are held up by Norman pillars. The nave is wider than it is long. The font is ancient, and has a 17th century cover."

Buried in the churchyard is one of the most famous Victorian astronomers, Sir Norman Lockyer. 'His' observatory, first opened in 1913, is on the hill high above Sidmouth, and well worth a visit.

From the church walk up the road, signposted to Sidmouth. This is a steep incline which runs past Rock Cottage. Higher up the hill the road passes Combe Head and, above this, the entrance to Allotment Field Woods. Ignore this option to reach the war memorial on the junction at the top of the hill. Here turn right and immediately turn left onto a footpath leading off into a field. A

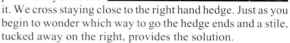

pillar tells you about it. We cross staying close to the right hand hedge. Just as you begin to wonder which way to go the hedge ends and a stile, tucked away on the right, provides the solution.

Cross it and head through the woods for about 100 yards until a footpath sign is reached. Instead of following its direction pass to the right of it, limbo dancing under the branches of a small, but angled, tree to reach a stile which we cross.

The way is now downhill and steep. It's tailor-made for downhill skiers but those with bad balance will have to proceed with caution. Much lower down the hillside a metal gateway is passed through as another path joins from the right. We continue onwards and downwards, leaving the woods behind to enjoy a grassy corridor downhill which soon becomes a surfaced road. At the bottom of the lane, we discover that this is Griggs Lane and here we turn left onto the road. This is Fortescue, a hamlet astride this thoroughfare which runs into Sidmouth but, unlike cars and other traffic, we can afford to take the scenic route back to the resort. About a hundred yards along we will see a clearly signed footpath off to the right. This is at the point where Fortescue Road ends and Sid Road begins. We turn right to descend the slope past Meadowside and pass through the gate to reach a footbridge over the River Sid, just below a small waterfall. The Sid is not a long river but it has a steep profile and from this point to the sea, a distance of only about one and a quarter miles, it drops some 80 feet. As you would expect, speeding Sid has several more waterfalls and we will see them in due course.

Beyond the footbridge the path first gently veers away from the river and then passes through a gate, originally painted blue, to head off at a right angle.

In about 100 yards a crossroads of paths is met and, luxury of luxuries, the public footpath that we take (left) is surfaced.

The combination of nearby houses, part of the resort's inevitable sprawl along its valley, and the user-friendly lack of gradient, means that this, 'The Byes', is prime dog-walking country. Bear this in mind and show due care and attention when walking the next mile or so. Beside the path

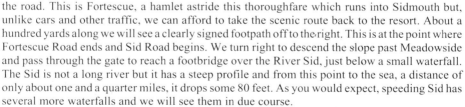

is a dry ditch which looks like a dried-up mill leat. Our path, with fields and hills to the left, and houses to the right, eventually crosses this shallow depression. Stay with the general direction you are travelling now. The path runs, for a short while, between hedgerows but soon emerges into an attractive parkland setting. A small stream comes in from the right to join the Sid at this point. This is the Wool Brook and gives its name to the 'Higher', 'Lower' and 'Middle Woolbrook' districts of the town. A small bridge guarantees our safe passage over it.

The first of a large number of park benches is met; almost every single one is dedicated and many reflect the love felt for Sidmouth. This one is "In loving memory of F. B. & G. W. Sparshott".

Soon a National Trust sign, on our left, informs us that this is Sid Meadow and open to the public subject to bye-laws. Just beyond there is a well-constructed footbridge over the river, which we cross only to continue our journey down stream. The presence of trees and grassy meadows helps to disguise the fact that we are now in the heart of the resort. Observant wayfarers will notice that the banks, in several places, are shored up by the placement of enormous boulders, evidence that this pretty watercourse, with its ducks and other forms of wildfowl, occasionally reveals its meaner face.

We pass the Sid's own small-scale version of 'Niagara Falls' to reach a former tollhouse, with its tollgate beside it. If you want to know more about it then you should read *Sidmouth Past & Present*. Here there is also a Sid Valley Association 'information post', for want of a better tag. 'The Byes', the name given to this lowland Sid valley corridor, is believed to be a name derived from Somerset and the definition which has been suggested is 'The corners and ends of a field which cannot be reached by the plough, and must be dug by the hand.'

Carefully cross over the road and head on down Millford Road, with its flint-encrusted houses, dating back to about 1909, until a ford is reached where the depth of the river is marked off in feet. Here, provided the river is not a 'speeding Sid' and in full spate, drivers can wash the lower parts of their cars as they traverse the watery obstacle. We, though, are spared the chilling experience because a footbridge sees us safely over to the far bank. This is our fourth, and last, crossing of the river on this walk.

We are now in Mill Street. After about 80 yards we come upon a small triangular car park. However before we meet it we turn left into Riverside Road which takes us beside the river even though we can't see it. However we can see the deep red river cliffs beyond it. At the end of the road is a playpark, which we walk through to reach the end of the walk where we started an hour or two ago. But first we pay brief homage to John George Gallaway Bradford Esq. who gave this open space for recreation on 26 March 1896, over a century ago.

We have seen country and coast and glimpses along the way help to show us how important the Sid valley has been in the shaping of the resort and, more to the point, we have had an extremely easy last mile or two to make up for that first 'struggle'!

3: Up Peak Hill and Back Down Again!

This is a walk of about three miles which starts and finishes at the Tourist Information Centre. There is one long climb which, for those in need, is punctuated by the placement of benches along the way. Therefore it's possible to take regular breaks on the ascent of the east face of Peak Hill, if your old engine is not as efficient as it may have once been. Again, the second half of the walk is 'a doddle'...

From the Tourist Information Centre stroll the short distance to the eastern end of Sidmouth's historic sea front, one which will reveal itself to you as you pass along it walking westwards. It was at this eastern end of the sea front that the *Duchess of Devonshire* went aground in 1934. (It should be stressed that this was a ship, not a titled lady!) In the ensuing years she was broken up and from time to time fragments of her are found here.

The route instructions for the time being are quite basic: the sea is to your left; the line of buildings, mostly hotels, holiday apartments and restaurants, which forms the impressive Esplanade, is to your right.

In the morning sunshine of a fine spring, summer or even autumn day this interface between the land and sea which is 'forever England' is a place where people commune with nature, and it's quite a common sight to see folk, even those who have had a good night's sleep, with eyelids shuttered tight and mouths agape as they relax in sleepy Sidmouth. Please avoid the temptation to awake them from their slumbers. I don't think they would take too kindly to an invitation to join you on this walk!

A stone bearing a plaque commemorates the efforts of those who struggled during the first half of the 1990s to build the resort's latest sea defences. Over the years Sidmouth has taken a number of batterings from the elements and the story of its beach has been very much a case of 'Now you see me...' Hopefully when you do this walk all will be peaceful and calm, and you may well wonder what all the fuss was about. However, if you have any doubts the owners of the sea-front properties would be the first to tell you how horrendous conditions can become along this fickle foreshore.

For those who like trivia, this sea front has been used at various times for attempts to beat the world conga record so, if you feel like getting in some practice ...

It doesn't take long to reach the western end of the sea front, near the unusual arch to the Belmont Hotel, unless, of course, there is a stiff wind blowing into your face.

Where the sea front abruptly stops there is a short causeway, to its right, down onto the beach. Making sure you don't cause an obstruction, head down it and along the top of the beach for a short distance. You will notice some attractive thatched properties high above you. At the base of the cliffs a short flight of steps carries you onto a walkway which leads beneath the Connaught Gardens, named after the Duke of that name who performed the opening ceremony in 1934. It is obvious that the sea has undermined these cliffs and shoring-up works have been made to secure the cliff face. If the tide is out, away to your left is an extensive area of rock pools, Chit Rocks. There used to be one isolated, throne-like rock where fishermen would perform an annual ritual of crowning one of their number 'King of Chit', but storm waves have long accounted for this red sandstone stack.

Follow this pathway beneath the cliffs until it reaches its end as it turns the corner to reach the base of Jacob's Ladder, the third structure in this location to bear the name. It was featured in H. G. Wells' *The Sea Raiders*.

From this point a chine or cutting in the cliffs enables you to ascend a zig-zag route. Above you, on a raised shelf, are eight benches, a reminder, if one was needed, that in so beautiful a place most folks are simply content to sit, enjoy the surroundings and 'watch the world go by'. This they do by the kind courtesy of the friends and relations of those named on these seats, most of which carry some sort of message recording the affection that those remembered had for Sidmouth.

Climb up the chine and then head left onto the green corridor which separates the coast road to Otterton from the cliff-top. It resembles a golf fairway and marks the start, for us, of the real long climb which will ultimately take us to the top of Peak Hill. However the going underfoot is grassy and fairly firm and if we don't rush it the exercise will do us good. A bench in the centre of the 'fairway' offers an opportunity to sit and look back over Sidmouth and along the coastline eastwards towards Beer Head. (Should this bench be occupied there are at least ten others set back from the cliff-top above it.)

The green corridor ends when we pass through a gap in a hedge. On your left is another vantage point where there is good view westwards towards Ladram Bay, marked in this view by sea-stacks off it. We are now opposite the entrance to Flint House and Foxes Corner, both names, no doubt, appropriate to their situations. Certainly flints are found extensively in this district.

We bear left and upwards again. Here there is evidence of coastal erosion. A short section of the old road to Otterton subsided some years ago and a new section was hastily built because of the great inconvenience that its closure caused. We now walk part of that old road but at its start stop in the gateway to see a memorial to that wonderful writer Ronnie Delderfield (1912–1972). He wrote a number of novels that were bought by television companies and dramatised. These included *To Serve Them All My Days,* based on Delderfield's experiences as a schoolmaster at West Buckland School, near South Molton, and *A Horseman Riding By,* another terrific book and series. Both were filmed in Devon. The reason for this choice of location for a memorial is that Ronnie lived here, at the 'Gazebo', just at the top of this short section of old road.

Close to this memorial is another sign which informs us that the field beyond the more newly-built road is Willoughby Field (not 'Filed' as on the sign!). It is owned by the East Devon District Council and is being managed by grazing without the use of inorganic or organic fertilisers. 'The objective is to protect and enhance the range of plant life together with the associated invertebrate interest. Specific management is undertaken to control the invasive plant known as Giant Hogweed'.

Walk up the short bit of old road and on reaching the far gateway, by 'The Gazebo', head on up the existing road, past Peak Cottage with its neat gateposts, for a short distance. Almost opposite the entrance to Willoughby House, and on the left side of the road, is a footpath which we take. This is the start of a long staircase and unless we are either a giant or a dwarf the steps mean we have to ascend with our gait impeded, such is the interval in them. However, whoever put them there did so for our benefit and they make the sharpest part of our ascent a little easier, particularly if this walk is done after a period of prolonged heavy rain, when the ground conditions can be decidedly soft and slippery. Tyre marks are evidence of the occasional presence of mountain bikers so keep a wary eye out for these daredevils!

This stairway takes us to the cliff-edge once more and another view towards Ladram Bay. Ignore a path marked off to the right because that leads back to the road we have just left. Just beyond the bench dedicated to Freda Bartlett (1911–1960) is a NT sign telling us of our arrival on Peak Hill. Stay with the path, which wends a short distance away from the cliff-top before heading back towards it again. Soon the woods thin out and a much more open aspect presents itself as the upper tier of this hill is reached. We pass through a kissing gate but stifle our own passion to read yet another

sign. "This land forms part of Pinn Barton Farm situated..." but you can read, learn and enjoy for yourself this time! At this point it is time for us to head inland, almost at a right angle to the line of the coast. A discernible path of sorts runs through the greensward and maintains a course parallel to the right hand hedge. Away to the right there are views over the lower Otter valley and beyond but to your left the views are restricted by the woods of Peak Hill. After several hundred yards a muddy gateway is passed through and in a short distance our old friend, the Sidmouth–Otterton road, is met again at another kissing gate. Carefully cross over it and if you are extremely tall take care to duck as you enter the car park. Head to the noticeboard and take in its contents. A trackway leads away to

the right of it, 'Public Bridleway Bulverton Hill 1¼ miles', onto land of the Clinton Devon Estates. This is reached by crossing Mutter's Moor, a name derived from a local family who were 'occasionally' involved in smuggling!

On your right you will now find woodland whilst on your left is the rough and almost impenetrable heathland, a rich wildlife habitat. The way ahead is almost flat and the conditions underfoot are generally good, so good in fact that many walk this way. After about 500 yards a gateway is met on the right. Here, behind the hedge, is a small hut made of concrete blocks. This is mentioned simply to help confirm your exact whereabouts. There is a signpost complete with three arrows. The direction which we want is shown by the yellow arrow. Turn right here. Access into the woodland of Greystone Hill Plantations is by a narrow gap to the left of the gate. Breath in and, hopefully, you will pass through without hindrance. Once more we head almost at right angles to the last path we have followed. Initially the path is fairly level but soon, after passing over a crossroads of paths, we 'plunge over the edge of the hill'. A good sense of balance is essential to negotiate this downward slope. And if you are an experienced downhill skier and you fancy hurtling down this woodland scree slope, first bear in mind that there are a number of tree roots and flint stones protruding just above the surface of the ground! (I speak from experience!)

At the bottom of the steep section another path is met. Here we do not infringe on the privacy of the golf course but instead bear left down a heavily rutted and uneven track. In a short distance a single footpath sign seems to suggest that we head left and uphill again. Don't! Be contrary and continue right and downhill. We pass over the path leading to the sixth tee and descend to pass 'Woodlands Cottage'.

Stay on the road, which now has a much better surface. Ahead is the green oasis of the upper part of Bickwell Valley complete with the conglomeration of buildings of Bickwell Farm. It's hard to imagine that the coast and the resort of Sidmouth is so close at hand, as this scene has every appearance of being in the heart of the country. We reach a junction close to a house called 'Appletreewick', one which has palm trees at its entrance. Here turn right. Follow the road until a 30 mph sign is encountered. This marks the end of Muttersmoor Road and, as far as we are concerned, the end of open countryside.

Turn right into Bickwell Valley, once a countryside corridor but now the preserve of those with sufficient incomes to afford such fine homes. This is a long valley road but it's quiet. There is an overall slight drop towards sea level and there's a pavement on the right side for most of the way. If you are wondering where the stream has got to, it is there but seems shy of the public! The pavement runs out on the right hand side at the junction with Boughmore Road but continues on the left.

Soon Bickwell Valley is joined on the left by Convent Road but ignore the temptation and, with or without a vow of silence, head on down the road for a short way. Cotmaton Road cuts across Bickwell Valley and it's here we take our leave of the route that we have followed for almost half a mile.

We turn left to be immediately impressed by an older property, the wonderful and aptly-named 'The White Cottage'. Its neighbour is Cotmaton Cottage, another excellent example of the cottage *orné* style of architecture so common in this classy resort. Just beyond Cheese Lane, which joins us from the left, a stream issues from the wall. This follows our road and was probably the feed to a well, now drier than Arizona, that lies on the left hand side of the road a short way ahead. The words 'Sidmouth Parish' can still be read on it.

On reaching Seafield Road turn right. Almost immediately one of the famous blue plaques, so useful to visitors with a quest for local knowledge, is found on the right hand side. This marks the site of Cotmaton Old Hall, which was destroyed by fire. It was a thatched residence and its lands extended right up the slopes of Peak Hill where we walked earlier in this outing.

Seafield Road immediately curves around to the left to give us a view, dead straight ahead, of Sidmouth's parish church. Our route, which will soon pass it, almost follows a straight line towards it. At the next junction you will notice the unusual and attractive Pebblestone Cottage on your left. Taking care, cross straight over the road and walk down Coburg Road. If you are observant you will again notice the attractive cottages along this road, all from a period when the resort boasted many important visitors from various royal families around the world.

Sidmouth's fine museum sits at the end of Coburg Road and, turning the corner beside it, we enter Church Street, one that we could have probably guessed its name even if a nameplate hadn't informed us. In a short distance Market Square is met and those in need of the toilets can seek solace here.

Bear right and past the Market PO to reach the sea front once again. Turn left and retrace your steps to the end of the walk at the Tourist Information Centre. A dip in the warm pool is a fine way to end a stroll, but take off your walking boots first!

4: A Sidford Safari

This lovely circular walk starts from the free car park in Sidford but there is one slight drawback: the parking time limit is two hours during the working day from Monday to Saturday. The walk is about four miles and two hours should be long enough so there might not be a problem. If you are the type who worries about such a constraint then park in one of the side streets, but show consideration to the residents.

Leave the car park the way you drove in. At the main road turn right, towards Seaton, and walk down the road. On your left is St Peter's Church and on your right the Salty Monk.

Carefully cross the road here and head on to Sidford Bridge, where a little humpback bridge carries you over the River Sid. Joining it here is a tributary, the Snod Brook, which plays its part in our ramble. Continue along the road until Harcombe Lane is reached on your left. Turn into it and walk along this thoroughfare, which is one of attractive bungalows with neat, colourful gardens and appropriate house names. It isn't a long road and soon a junction is met where we veer right of the bench placed there to the memory of Frederick T. Marsh, to travel on almost straight ahead towards Boswell Farm and Knowle House, now a retirement home.

This lane gives us our first taste of countryside as we leave Sidford behind to make our way up an attractive valley. Ahead to our left is Buckton Hill and later we shall descend from the top of it, but we have some calories to burn before that!

The Snod Brook runs closer to us as we pass along the lane to Boswell Farm. It's a fast flowing brook with a steep profile that results in miniature waterfalls and mini-rapids, albeit on a model-village scale of things. In spate this brook can sweep all before it and it is a major tributary of the Sid.

Boswell Farm is an attractive dwelling just beyond the Snod Brook and we pass it as we gently rise towards Knowle House. Beyond it the stream is ponded back and beyond that we pass over a cattle grid as the hedges give way to a more open prospect. We pass to the right of the stone-pillared gateway of Knowle and, after a short curving rise of about 50 yards, we reach a signpost which shepherds us off to the left and along a lane. At the second gateway, a wooden one, a path leads off left down a short drop to a footbridge spanning the Snod Brook. Beyond is a row of cottages and the path, a rough one, veers to the right of them. Pass through the farm gate, of Harecombe Farm, once you have worked out how to open it, and ascend the gentle, short slope to the road.

Here turn left but in just twenty yards turn right onto a track that climbs the hill. In a short distance there is a forking of the ways and you take the right one this time. Almost immediately is another choice of routes. This time continue straight ahead through the metal gate (but open it first). Some of the wetter parts of this lane have been infilled with stones, which is fine if you have some thickness in your sole to prevent them being felt underfoot.

I enjoyed the next half-mile or so because the path, easy on the feet, contoured the hill and provided views, in the direction of Harcombe, of this green and pleasant valley. But all good things come to an end and so it was with this as a small, almost nonexistent 'ford' was reached where the path, no doubt bored with gentle gradients, has decided to make life much tougher for its followers. At a blue arrow the path turns left to ascend the steep hill to a gate and a stile, a time to reflect on one's own physical shortcomings!

Beyond this stile the way ahead is not abundantly clear as a 'parkland' setting presents itself. About a hundred yards ahead and to the right there is an even steeper green slope, possibly the back wall of a former quarry. The path, which runs along above this scarp slope, is reached by ascending the hill to the left of this. When you reach it you will see more blue arrows and a path.

For the next half a mile the path dips into and out of the woods a number of times. There are places where the ground is soft and squelchy and others where progress is easy. It would be a dull task for me to record every gate that is passed through. Suffice it to say that the path, sometimes obvious, sometimes not, follows the hillside north-eastwards until it eventually meets a drier bolder cart-track near Lower Sweetcombe Farm. On reaching it maintain the same direction to pass through a rusty gate or two, above and to the left of this 'detached' building. This is a wonderfully sheltered place to live and in a marvellous setting, with the wooded upper part of the valley providing some striking scenery. I walked the path alone for this booklet and saw rabbits, squirrels, deer and a fox.

From this farm the track climbs steeply, bends sharply and rises to Wren's Nest, a modern bungalow with a view down the V-shaped valley to enjoy a glimpse of the sea. The farm track rises to about the highest point of the walk and here, on a plateau, we are on a similar level to other hilltops in East Devon. The views are not spectacular but the immediate countryside is glorious. Stay with the farm track until it reaches a road several hundred yards farther along. Turn left and descend what is the upper slope of Hatway Hill for about 200 yards. On the left is a clearly signposted bridleway which we turn onto and it becomes our corridor for the next stretch. The going is fairly level and easy underfoot, the sort of walking I enjoy as little concentration is necessary and the surroundings can be savoured.

After about half a mile the path opens into a small 'clearing' where a narrow path, shown by

yellow arrows, goes off to the right. Ignore it. Continue a short way ahead and climb the nearby stile into a large field. The way ahead is along its right hand edge for about 250 yards. This takes you, initially, past a small stable, a reminder that this is fine horse-riding country. At the end of the field re-enter the woodlands by passing through a gate. The track continues ahead and on the level for a while but swings right to descend very steeply from the heights of Buckton Hill. Where the track emerges from the wood there is an excellent view of the lower Sid Valley. Many of Sidmouth's landmarks can be spied and also the coastal cliffs near Ladram Bay. Away to the right Sidbury Castle, an ancient hill-fort, can be seen.

Buckton Farm is below you. Head to the hedge, down the slope to the right of the farm buildings, which will take you down to a road. Continue in the same direction and ignore the road to the right, the rough track ahead will return you to Sidford without a detour. It's all downhill for now and soon another road comes in from the right just before Harcombe Cross. Head on to Sidford by continuing on down the hill and over the Snod Brook. A short way up the next rise you may recognise the spot as the place we were at much earlier. Turn right into Harcombe Lane, and right again at the main road over the packhorse bridge, past St Peter's Church to return to your car as the last seconds of your two-hour entitlement tick excitingly away as you reach the car park. Those 'sands of time' have been well-spent on this lovely circular walk, provided 'the yellow peril' doesn't lie in wait for you on your return!

5: A Rocky Ramble For All Ages!

This lovely walk starts at Harpford in the Otter valley and a few miles from the edge of Sidmouth. However, along the way there are views, down the valley, of the resort. Park sensibly near the beautiful church of St Gregory the Great. A one-time vicar of this church was the Rev Augustus Montague Toplady, writer of the famous hymn 'Rock of Ages', and it's possible, but unlikely, that his inspiration for it is found on our walk of about 4 miles.

From the war memorial, at the road junction, on the corner of the churchyard, walk northwards along the road for the shortest of distances until another road, Knapps Lane, leads off to the right. Turn right onto this and on your right is the attractively thatched property called Littlecott. Beyond it you enter a fern-filled sandstone cutting. If you are observant you will now note a wooden sign on a gate which spells 'Littlecot' with a single 't' at the end, so perhaps along the way it has dropped off!

At the signpost, which says 'Bowd 1M', head straight on as we are Bowd-bound. Here we are on part of the 'East Devon Way' route, a long distance path opened in the 1990s. Initially there are one or two wet places along this lane but nothing that a sturdy pair of boots can't take in their stride. The lane is following a valley and curves round to reach the stream which flows through it. When I did this walk its bed was dry but in the stream's upper reaches there was water. This is most unusual as Devon streams never seem to run dry like those of neighbouring Dorset, where the geology often produces 'bournes' which dry up in summer when the water table drops.

The path enters Harpford Wood, a curious and splendid wonderland. After a 'long' quarter-mile a point is reached where a choice has to made on which way to proceed. A narrow path rises up a steep slope to our left whilst two paths head onwards on a more level course. You can take either of the latter for both will reach the same point in a few hundred yards. The left of the two is the more obvious track.

The very steep scarp slope, or embank-ment, on the left has the old railway track between Tipton and Sidmouth on top of it. This short branch line opened on 6 July 1874 and ran from the Otter valley, through these woods, on an incline to 'Bowd Summit', to drop down to the edge of Sidmouth. The last passenger train rumbled through these woods on 6 March 1967 so if you hear locomotive noises … it's a ghost train!

Both paths rejoin where a culvert emerges on the left from under that slope. We head straight on and in a few yards see a small, but impressive waterfall, complete with plunge pool, Harpford Wood's own 'Niagara Falls'! The streams through this wood have exposed bluffs of bare rock in many places, here capped with orange rocks giving way to redder ones below. Who knows whether the rocks were more obvious when the Rev Toplady (1740–1778) wandered through here in the eighteenth century. Could his 'Rock of Ages' have been inspired by this woodland wonderland? The popular belief is that it was Somerset's Ebbor Gorge, a few miles from Cheddar, which is where he took shelter from a thunderstorm as the hymn formed itself in his mind.

Immediately, within about 30 yards, we have another choice of paths, a common occurrence in woods like this. Bear right to climb over a small knoll before returning to follow the small stream again through a narrow cleft.

After a few hundred yards the path veers left to leave the stream and climb up to the road at the hamlet of Bowd. Should you require refreshment there is a fine pub just a few yards to the right of where we join the road. However, if you want to stay with the walk take great care at this junction to turn left over the former railway bridge and immediately right to walk up Fire Beacon Lane.

Most of the properties on the right of this lane reflect nature or topography in the lane so we stroll purposefully past Oaklands, Edgefield, Westwoods, The Laurels, Dovedale, Plum Cottage and Selworthy to reach the bend of the road at Saltways. Here we head straight on along the road which will become, for us, a public footpath. But first we pass Thatchby and later Greenacres to weave our way past some farm buildings and an impressive modern house to reach a gate to an open field. Ahead is a tree bearing a small yellow arrow which confirms that we are on the right route. The path now heads straight across a large and uneven field and again, if you have keen eyesight, you may spy a stile on the far side of it. To your right and down the valley lies sleepy Sidmouth, blissfully unaware of those strolling about in the hills all around it. Back over your shoulder is a fine view of Bulverton Hill, a wooded and impressive eminence.

Cross the stile and turn left along the lane. Immediately there is another choice but continue onwards up this sunken path, possibly an old cattle drovers' route.

Higher up the hedges on either side stop. Here bear right and in about 50 yards, just beyond a ditch/stream, is yet another stile which we cross, and another field to traverse.

Beyond the next stile is a road. Turn left, and 'walk uphill' is the theme of the next quarter of a mile. Ahead you will see two road signs 'Except for agricultural access'. Head between them and walk up this long, steep but pleasantly wooded corridor. Almost at the brow of the hill, and through a gap on the right, is a memorial to a man who loved these woods.

We stay with this track for a few hundred yards further, now much easier going, until a public footpath is clearly signed to the left. Take it and soon the much more open environment of Harpford Common is reached. In the peat there are all sorts of marks of motorbikes, bicycles and many animals' footprints. Sherlock Holmes would have a field day!

The path veers around the common and affords terrific views along the South Devon coastline, and headlands like Hope's Nose, and Sharkham Point beyond Brixham, are visible on a clear day. The small resort of Budleigh Salterton is also conspicuous, as are the various commons of Woodbury Common, the subject of another of my walking books. There are good views over Newton Poppleford, a village as long as its name!

Pass beneath some telegraph wires to reach a meeting place of paths. Our way is left and immediately right, a staggered junction for us. In a short distance a T-junction is met by woods, Fire Beacon Plantation. Turn left here and descend the hill past some tall scrubland, gorse vegetation. The path then veers left and starts to drop more steeply downwards. Stay with the main path, now stony, which descends from the heights of Harpford Common by cutting across the side of the hill and under the telegraph wires once more. This means that the gradient is less severe and the brakes do not have to be applied.

After a few more hundred yards of descent a point, at the bottom of the steepest part of Fire Beacon Hill, is reached where a great many paths and tracks join. Here we almost double back on ourselves to turn right. Although this takes us slightly uphill again it's not too vertically challenging!

Soon this narrow path, having passed the telegraph poles for the third and last time, brings us around and down onto a road. Turn right and in about 70 yards descend by a footpath sign to enter an immense field. The way out of it is at the bottom where the road runs. Descend the field towards

Harpford Wood and locate some stiles at the bottom. The way, once the road is safely crossed, is straight on, over another stile and into the woods.

After 20 yards bear left and in another 40 yards, where there is an obvious fork, bear right. In another few hundred pleasant yards is another choice of tracks. This time bear left and head downhill, a yellow arrow pointing the way. Soon this drops more steeply down to reach a point where the former railway line is encountered yet again. Pass under it and bear right. In no time you will recognise that we are back at our 'Niagara Falls'.

The rest is a repeat, in reverse of course, of what we did earlier. The route is straight ahead and either of the two paths can be taken. By now keeping the stream on your left, the way back to Harpford is straightforward, so civilisation will be regained in about half a mile. The 'Rock of All Ages', just cleft for us today, will soon be left behind.